No One

Saves You

But

Yourself

Dr. W. Koros

For every reader who dares to journey inward.

Acknowledgements

With gratitude to my family, mentors, and readers, your quiet strength, encouragement, and belief continue to make these words possible.

Contents

Introduction: The Lonely Truth

At some point in your life, you will look around and realize that no one is coming.

Not your parents, not your friends, not your government, not your partner, not even the gods you pray to in secret. The cavalry you keep imagining, the one that will burst over the hill and pull you out of your suffering, is a mirage.

Most people waste years of their lives waiting for that cavalry. They wait for someone to finally understand them. They wait for luck to finally tip in their favor. They wait for the world to hand them permission to live. And all the while, time keeps moving, and the quiet truth sits in the corner like a shadow:

No one saves you but yourself.

This truth can feel like a curse. It strips away the comfort of blame and the illusions of rescue. It forces you into the terrifying awareness that your survival, your dignity, and your progress they all live or die by your own hands.

But if you can stand in this truth without flinching, you will discover that it is not a curse at all. It is liberation.

Because if no one else is responsible for saving you, then no one else has the power to stop you.

This book is not about hope in the conventional sense. It is not about waiting for miracles. It is about the long, difficult, often lonely work of becoming your own rescuer, of learning how to walk through fire without expecting someone else to carry you.

It is about taking ownership so completely that the world can no longer hold you hostage.

Part I:
The Illusion of Rescue

Chapter 1: The Childhood Promise

When you are a child, you are helpless, and that helplessness feels natural.

Someone feeds you, someone clothes you, someone tucks you into bed. If you cry, someone comes running. If you fall, someone picks you up. Childhood is built on the quiet assumption that someone else is in control, someone else is watching, someone else is responsible for your survival.

And at first, that's true.

But the danger comes when this assumption lingers long past its usefulness.

We are trained from the earliest years to look outward for rescue. Parents soothe our pain, teachers give us answers, doctors heal our wounds, and authorities enforce the rules. The message is subtle but relentless:

Don't worry, someone else will take care of it!

This conditioning runs deep. It creates a promise we carry into adulthood, the Childhood Promise:

If I am hurting, someone will save me. If I am lost, someone will guide me. If I am broken, someone will fix me.

It's a comforting story, but it is not reality.

As you grow older, the support scaffolding of childhood falls away. The teachers stop handing out gold stars, the world no longer applauds your effort just for showing up, and the people who once tucked you into bed become fallible, flawed, and preoccupied with their own survival.

For many, this moment is a shock. We discover that parents can't always protect us, partners won't always stay, governments don't always provide, and friends aren't always reliable. The cavalry doesn't come. And if you've built your life around the Childhood Promise, that realization can feel like betrayal.

But here's the secret no one tells you: it isn't betrayal. It's simply reality revealing itself.

The problem isn't that people fail you; the problem is believing it was ever their job to save you in the first place.

Breaking free from the Childhood Promise is one of the hardest steps you will ever take. It requires you to look at the structures of your life, the people, the systems, the beliefs, and admit that they are not built to carry you. They may walk beside you, they may lend you a hand, but they will not lift the weight for you.

That is your work. Always.

The moment you accept this, you begin to grow a new kind of strength, a strength that doesn't depend on rescue. It is the strength of the self-reliant, the ones who know that no matter how much help comes or doesn't come, the responsibility remains theirs.

This is not cynicism. This is freedom.

Because when you let go of the Childhood Promise, you stop waiting. And when you stop waiting, you start moving.

Chapter 2: The Cultural Lie

If the Childhood Promise whispers that someone will always come to save you, the culture you grow up in shouts it from the rooftops.

From the moment you can understand stories, you are fed tales of rescue. The princess is trapped in a tower, and a knight comes to save her. The hero is facing certain death, and a last-minute ally swoops in to pull them from the jaws of defeat. The world is in chaos, but a chosen one is destined to restore order.

These stories are beautiful, but they are also dangerous. They are not written to teach you how to survive; they are written to make you feel safe. They weave the Cultural Lie:

"When you are in trouble, someone will come."

It seeps into everything.

- Movies tell us that love will fix us.
- Religions promise that faith will save us.
- Politics assures us that leaders will deliver us.

- Advertisements suggest that products will transform us.

Everywhere you turn, the message is the same: *wait long enough, believe hard enough, buy the right thing, and your savior will appear.*

But real life doesn't follow that script.

In real life, the tower remains locked until you learn to break the door yourself. The battle doesn't turn because a hero arrives; it turns because you kept fighting long after you were exhausted. The world doesn't hand you redemption; you build it with blood, discipline, and persistence.

The Cultural Lie is so seductive because it allows you to avoid responsibility. If salvation is always external, then you never have to face the terrifying truth of your own power. You can sit still, point to the sky, and say, *"Any day now, they will come for me."*

But days turn into years. And years turn into decades.

Look closely at the people who believed the Cultural Lie for too long. You will find men and women who spent their lives waiting for love that never arrived, leaders who never delivered, or divine intervention that never materialized. They are left hollow, carrying both the weight of disappointment and the bitterness of betrayal.

The betrayal is real, but it was never the culture's job to tell you the truth. Culture's job is to soothe, to sell, to entertain, to control.

The truth is harsher, but it is also cleaner:

"No story will save you. You are not the character waiting for rescue; you are the author, and the pen is in your hand."

Once you see the Cultural Lie for what it is, you cannot go back. You cannot unsee the machinery of stories designed to keep you passive. And though this realization stings, it is the first cut of freedom.

Because the moment you stop looking for rescue in myths and promises, you begin to write your own script, one where the ending doesn't depend on anyone arriving.

Chapter 3: The Cost of Waiting

Waiting feels safe.

It allows you to postpone action. It gives you the illusion that time itself is working on your behalf, that if you just stay still long enough, someone or something will arrive to change your circumstances.

But waiting is not safety. Waiting is corrosion.

Every year you spend waiting for rescue, your muscles atrophy, not just the ones in your body, but the ones in your will. You learn helplessness. You begin to confuse passivity with patience, stagnation with faith, and surrender with wisdom. And slowly, without noticing, you begin to die long before your body does.

Consider the person who stays in a broken relationship because they are waiting for their partner to finally change.

Consider the employee who hates their job but tells themselves that "one day" the right opportunity will land in their lap.

Consider the dreamer who wants to write, paint, travel, or build, but spends years saying, *"I'm just waiting for the right time."*

They are all waiting for rescue. And in the meantime, life moves on without them.

The cost of waiting is not only lost time, it is lost power. Every moment you sit idle, hoping for a savior, you are silently training yourself to believe you have none. Your mind begins to whisper: *If I could have saved myself, I would have done it already. The fact that I am still here proves I cannot.*

This is how waiting becomes a prison. The longer you stay inside it, the harder it is to leave.

Worse still, life does not pause while you wait. Bills still arrive. Bodies still age. Opportunities still pass. Relationships still decay. The world does not hold still out of sympathy for your hesitation. And when you finally realize that no one is coming, you may discover that you have less strength and fewer options than you once had.

This is the great tragedy of waiting: not only does no one come, but by the time you accept that, you are weaker than when you began.

But here lies the paradox: while waiting eats away at your power, action builds it. Every small step you take on your own behalf is proof to yourself that you can. And proof compounds.

The person who finally leaves the toxic relationship discovers they can survive alone. The employee who takes a risk on a new path discovers they can create opportunities instead of waiting for them. The dreamer who sits down and begins their craft discovers that the "right time" was always when they started.

The difference between those who live and those who wither is not talent, luck, or divine favor. It is the willingness to stop waiting.

Because the truth is brutal but simple:

"No one is coming. The rescue you wait for is already inside you, and every day you delay is a day you betray it."

Part II:
The Hard Reality

Chapter 4: The Mirror Principle

Stand in front of a mirror. Look closely. That face staring back at you, tired, hopeful, angry, or afraid, is the only rescuer you will ever meet.

The Mirror Principle is simple, and it is ruthless:

"The only person responsible for your survival is the one in the reflection."

This truth unsettles people. Most would rather look anywhere else than in the mirror. It feels easier to assign responsibility outward: to parents who failed us, bosses who underpaid us, partners who left us, systems that oppressed us, or gods who stayed silent.

And there is truth in those stories. Parents do fail. Systems are cruel. Life is unfair. But none of that changes the Mirror Principle. Because no matter what was done to you, no matter what was withheld, no matter how unfair the hand you were dealt, the person in the mirror is still the only one who can change what happens next.

That truth can feel like a slap.

It strips away excuses. It removes the comfort of blame. It leaves you alone with the stark, terrifying realization: *if anything is going to change, it will be because I make it change.*

But here's the paradox: while this truth feels heavy at first, it is also the lightest freedom you will ever know.

Because when you finally accept the Mirror Principle, you stop waiting for the world to be different. You stop bargaining with fate, stop begging for fairness, stop looking outward for salvation. You take all that energy you once wasted on wishing and place it back where it belongs: into your own hands.

The reflection in the glass becomes your ally. You begin to look into your own eyes not with shame, but with responsibility. You realize that while no one else is coming, this person has been here all along. They have scars, yes, but they are still standing. They are battered, but not broken. They have carried you through every disaster so far, and they will carry you through the next one, if you let them.

The Mirror Principle demands courage. It demands that you stop lying to yourself about whose job it is to save you. But it also gives you back something that waiting and blame can never provide: **agency.**

When you fully understand the Mirror Principle, you realize there is no cavalry, no rescue, no savior. There is only you. And far from being a curse, this is your liberation.

Because if the only person responsible for your survival is the one in the reflection, then no one, not the past, not the system, not fate itself, can take that power away from you.

The mirror does not lie. And neither should you.

Chapter 5: The Abyss Within

The first time you truly accept that no one is coming, a silence settles over you. It is not the calm silence of peace; it is the heavy, suffocating silence of the abyss.

This abyss is not out there in the world. It lives inside you. It is the space between who you are and who you must become if you are to survive without rescue. And standing at its edge can feel unbearable.

Most people never face it. They turn away, running back to distractions, to noise, to the soothing promise that perhaps they are wrong, perhaps someone will still appear to save them. They drown themselves in work, in relationships, in substances, in entertainment, anything to avoid looking into the abyss.

But avoidance has a cost. Because what you avoid does not disappear. It waits. And the longer you delay, the darker it grows.

To confront the abyss within is to finally sit with your despair, your loneliness, your anger, and your fear without flinching. It is to realize that no cavalry is coming, and that even if they did, they could not erase what is inside you.

The abyss whispers cruel truths:

- *You are weaker than you thought.*
- *You are more alone than you wanted to believe.*
- *You are afraid, and no one can feel that fear for you.*

But here is the secret most people never discover: the abyss does not only contain despair. It also contains your rawest strength.

When you sit with your fear long enough, you discover courage.

When you face your loneliness without numbing it, you uncover resilience.

When you admit your despair without running, you find a will that is harder than steel.

The abyss strips you down to nothing, and in that nothingness, you begin to see what cannot be taken from you.

It is not a pleasant process. It feels like death, because in many ways it is: the death of illusions, the death of dependency, the death of the self that believed rescue was guaranteed. But every death clears the ground for something new.

Those who dare to face the abyss emerge changed. They are not necessarily happier, but they are stronger, sharper, more real. They carry a kind of quiet fire, the fire of someone who has looked into the emptiness and decided to keep walking anyway.

And here is the paradox: the abyss you feared would destroy you becomes the place where you are reforged.

It will not happen overnight. Some days you will sit at the edge and want to turn back. Some days you will fall in and feel like you are drowning. But each time you return, each time you refuse to run, you carve a path through the darkness. And one day, you look around and realize that the abyss no longer terrifies you.

Because it is not a void anymore, it is the forge where you learned to save yourself.

Chapter 6: Rock Bottom as the Teacher

There is a point where everything falls apart.

Your plans collapse. Your strength fails. The scaffolding you leaned on, the job, the relationship, the health, the illusions, crumble in your hands. You are left standing in the wreckage, stripped of excuses and stripped of comfort. This is what people call *"Rock bottom."*

Most fear it like death. And in a way, they are right, it is a kind of death. The death of the old life, the death of the old self, the death of every illusion that you could get by without changing. But beneath the terror, there is something else hidden inside rock bottom, something most people overlook: **clarity**.

When you have nothing left, you see what is real.

At rock bottom, you can no longer afford lies. You cannot pretend that someone will save you, because if that were true, you would not be here. You cannot pretend that you have infinite time, because every wasted hour has brought you closer to this collapse.

You cannot pretend you are powerless, because if you do, you will not rise.

Rock bottom removes the masks. It takes away the distractions, the comforts, the false rescues you used to lean on. It leaves you naked with the truth: *if you are going to get up, it will be because you choose to get up.*

This is why rock bottom, though brutal, is also a teacher.

It teaches you what actually matters. When you have lost everything, the noise falls away, and the essentials reveal themselves. What you thought you needed, approval, applause, permission, is gone. What remains is survival, dignity, and the quiet will to move forward.

It teaches you humility. No matter how strong you believed you were, rock bottom reminds you that you are human, fragile, and fallible. And in that humility, a new kind of strength begins to grow, one that is rooted not in arrogance, but in endurance.

And most of all, rock bottom teaches you that you are stronger than you believed.

The fact that you are still breathing, even when everything has collapsed, is proof that you can endure more than you thought. Rock bottom is not the end. It is the foundation. The ground is hard, yes, but it is also solid. And from that ground, you can build again.

Many people never reach their true power because they never allow themselves to hit bottom. They cling to the edges, to half-truths, to crutches, afraid to fall. But those who have fallen, those who have shattered and rebuilt, carry a strength that cannot be faked.

They know that the worst has already happened, and still they are here.

If you are at rock bottom now, you may not believe this. You may feel only the weight of despair. But listen closely: what feels like the end is the beginning. You are standing at the threshold of your own rebirth.

The ground beneath you is hard enough to build on. And the person who will rise from this place will not be the same as the one who fell. They will be sharper, truer, more unbreakable.

Rock bottom is the cruelest teacher. But it is also the most honest.

Part III:

The Inner Revolution

Chapter 7: Forging the Will

When you first begin to rise from collapse, you quickly learn a brutal truth: motivation is a liar.

Motivation is fickle. It shows up when things are exciting, when you are fresh, when the dream feels near. But when the weight is heavy, when the nights are long, when the work is dull or the path uncertain, motivation vanishes. If you depend on it, you will collapse again.

What you need instead is will.

Will is different from motivation. Motivation is a spark; will is the fire you keep alive when the spark is gone. Motivation says, *"I want to."* Will says, *"I will, whether I want to or not."*

Forging the will is the heart of self-rescue. Without it, you are at the mercy of moods, of circumstance, of weather, of whether or not the world claps for you. With it, you can move forward even when everything in you screams to stop.

But will is not given; it is forged. And the forge is discipline.

Discipline is the repeated choice to act in service of what matters, even when you do not feel like it. Every time you act despite resistance, you hammer another strike into the steel of your will. Over time, those strikes shape something unbreakable.

Consider the small daily choices:

- Waking up when you said you would, even if the bed is warm.
- Showing up to train, even when your body aches.
- Writing the page, making the call, doing the work, even when no one is watching.

Each of these is a hammer blow. Small on its own, but powerful in accumulation.

The danger is waiting for the perfect moment. Too many waste years saying, *"I'll start when I feel ready."* But readiness never comes. You become ready by beginning before you feel ready, by acting before you believe you can, by moving before you trust the ground.

Every act of discipline is proof: proof that you are not ruled by moods, proof that you can command yourself, proof that you can be trusted with your own survival. And that proof builds the kind of self-respect no external savior can give.

Forging the will is not glamorous. There are no applause breaks, no heroic music, no crowds cheering. It is a slow grind, a quiet persistence. But over time, it creates something priceless: the ability to keep moving, even in darkness.

And once you have that, you are dangerous. Because a person with will cannot be stopped by lack of motivation, by lack of applause, or even by lack of hope, they move because they decided to move, and that is enough.

The world does not belong to the motivated. It belongs to the disciplined.

This is how you save yourself: not with bursts of inspiration, but with the steady, relentless hammer of will.

Chapter 8: Weapons of the Self

Once you begin forging the will, you discover something important: raw willpower alone is not enough.

Willpower is like a muscle, it tires, it burns out, it cannot hold forever. If you depend only on will, you will eventually collapse. To survive, you need tools. You need weapons you can reach for when the world is heavy and your strength is thin.

These weapons are not external. They are the habits, rituals, and mental tools you build into your life. They are the systems that carry you when your own energy falters.

Think of them as armor and blades for the inner war.

1. Habits: The Automations of Survival

Habits are decisions you no longer need to make. Instead of asking, *"Will I do this today?"* you simply do it. This removes the weight of choice, and in hard times, choice is what breaks people.

If you make exercise a habit, you no longer debate whether to move. You move.

If you make saving money a habit, you no longer wrestle with impulse. You save.

If you make creating a habit, you no longer wait for inspiration. You create.

The power of habits is not in their size, but in their persistence. A small habit repeated daily beats a grand effort attempted once.

2. Rituals: Anchors in Chaos

Where habits automate, rituals anchor. A ritual is a chosen act that centers you, reminding you of who you are and what you stand for.

It could be a morning routine that sharpens your focus.
It could be a nightly reflection that empties your mind of noise.

It could be as simple as lighting a candle before you write, or taking three deep breaths before you act.

Rituals seem small, but in times of chaos, they are lifelines. They remind you that even when the world is out of control, you are not.

3. Mindsets: The Shields Against Defeat

What you believe in the face of hardship determines whether you rise or break. This is where mindset becomes a weapon.

- **"Everything is training."** Instead of asking why hardship comes, you treat it as practice. Every obstacle is a weight that strengthens you.

- **"Pain is not the enemy."** Discomfort is not a signal to stop; it is a sign that you are growing.

- **"I am responsible."** Blame is seductive but weak. Responsibility is harsh but powerful. When you claim it, you reclaim control.

Mindsets are not slogans. They are stances. They change the way you carry yourself into the fight.

Together, these three weapons, habits, rituals, and mindsets make you more than willpower alone. They build a fortress around your discipline. They make it harder to fall, and easier to rise when you do.

The person who arms themselves with these tools becomes formidable. They do not rely on external rescue because their very life is structured to protect them from collapse.

You do not need to be perfect. You do not need to carry every weapon flawlessly. But you must carry something. Because the war within you is constant, and walking into battle unarmed is no longer an option.

Save yourself by building your arsenal. Because no one is coming to fight for you, and the war is already here.

Chapter 9: The Practice of Walking Alone

Walking alone is not a punishment. It is not a curse. It is a practice, one of the hardest, yet most liberating disciplines a person can undertake.

Most people fear solitude. They fill their lives with noise, company, distractions, and constant stimulation. To be alone, they believe, is to be abandoned. And in a way, it is, abandoned by the illusion that someone will save you.

But in that abandonment lies freedom.

When you walk alone, you are forced to rely entirely on yourself. No one carries your burdens. No one validates your progress. No one rescues you from your mistakes. Every step you take, every decision you make, is yours alone.

This practice builds independence. It teaches you to trust your own judgment. It teaches you to find comfort in your own presence. And most importantly, it shows you that you are enough, not because others say so, but because you have survived yourself.

Solitude also clarifies purpose. Noise is a mask. The company is a distraction. When you strip those away, what remains is the raw, unfiltered truth of your life. Your fears, your desires, your goals, your strengths, and your weaknesses all stand in stark relief. And when you face them without flinching, you begin to see the path forward with precision.

Walking alone does not mean you abandon connection. It means you stop depending on others to validate your worth or rescue you from hardship. It means relationships are no longer crutches, but choices. You can walk beside others without leaning on them. You can love without expecting salvation.

This is the paradox of solitude: it is both lonely and empowering. It is both hard and liberating. Those who master it do not simply survive; they move through the world with a quiet strength that cannot be shaken.

The practice is daily. It begins with small moments: a walk without your phone, a meal alone, a task completed without applause. Over time, it grows: entire projects, journeys, and decisions undertaken without external support.

And with practice, walking alone becomes natural. You no longer fear the silence. You no longer search for rescue. You no longer depend on anyone but yourself.

Because in the end, no one saves you but yourself, and when you walk alone, fully aware of this, you discover that you are already more powerful than you ever imagined.

Part IV:

Building a Life without Rescuers

Chapter 10: Self-Reliant Relationships

Independence does not mean isolation. Walking alone teaches strength, but humans are not meant to exist entirely apart. The challenge is learning to connect without surrendering your self-rescue. This is the art of self-reliant relationships.

A self-reliant relationship is one where each person stands on their own, yet chooses to walk together. No one carries the other. No one rescues the other. Support exists, yes, but it is mutual, not dependent. It is a partnership, not a lifeboat.

Most relationships fail because they are built on dependency. People lean on each other to fill gaps in their courage, stability, or happiness. And when one person falters, as inevitably they do, the other collapses too. It is a fragile architecture, prone to destruction.

Self-reliant relationships are different. Each person has already learned to save themselves. Each person has faced the abyss, forged their will, and armed themselves with the weapons of self. They come together not because they need rescue, but because they choose to share the journey.

This kind of connection is rare because it is demanding. It requires honesty. It requires boundaries. It requires self-knowledge.

You cannot walk beside someone if you do not know how to walk alone. You cannot love someone without expecting them to fix you.

Yet when it works, it is powerful. These relationships do not drain. They amplify. They create space for growth. They are not fragile boats tossed on a stormy sea; they are companions navigating the storm together, each with their own strength intact.

You begin to see the difference when you stop expecting others to save you:

- Arguments no longer feel like existential threats.
- Disagreements do not feel like abandonment.
- Absence does not feel like betrayal.

Instead, you feel choice, respect, and clarity. You love freely, because your happiness does not depend on theirs. You care fiercely because you are not afraid to lose them.

And you connect deeply, because connection is now a luxury of choice, not a crutch.

Self-reliant relationships are a mirror of the self you've forged. They reflect strength without demanding weakness, closeness without dependency, and loyalty without surrender.

The people who can walk alone and still choose companionship are the ones who truly live. They know that no one saves them, but they also know the richness of walking together anyway.

Chapter 11: Freedom and Responsibility

Freedom is a word often misunderstood. Most people think of it as the absence of constraints, the ability to do whatever you want, whenever you want. But true freedom is not granted. It is claimed. And it comes with a price: **responsibility.**

The deeper the freedom, the heavier the responsibility. If no one saves you, then you alone carry the consequences of every choice. Every action, every inaction, every failure, and every triumph rests squarely on your shoulders.

Many shrink from this responsibility. They trade freedom for the comfort of dependency: a boss to blame, a partner to hold accountable, a system to shield them. But this is not freedom. It is borrowed safety. And borrowed safety is fragile.

True freedom is paradoxical: it is terrifying and liberating at the same time. When you embrace it, you stop waiting for rescue. You stop asking for permission. You stop hoping that someone will make your life better.

Instead, you make it better yourself.

This is not easy. Freedom without responsibility is chaos. But responsibility without freedom is slavery. When you claim both, you step into a power that few ever experience. You are no longer a passenger. You are the driver. You are no longer a spectator. You are the author.

Responsibility sharpens clarity. Every decision becomes meaningful. Every act carries weight. And paradoxically, that weight gives you strength, purpose, and direction.

The person who saves themselves understands that freedom is not doing what they want, but doing what must be done. It is not an escape from obligations, but mastery over them. It is not permission to act recklessly, but authority to act decisively.

When you embrace freedom with responsibility, you also embrace your own life in full. You accept that you will stumble, that you will fail, and that you will face consequences alone. And in accepting this, you gain something priceless: the unshakable knowledge that you are capable of carrying yourself through anything.

No one saves you. You save yourself. And that is the foundation of freedom.

Chapter 12: No One Saves You but Yourself, and That's Good News

You have walked through the fire. You have faced the abyss. You have risen from rock bottom. You have forged your will, armed yourself with habits, rituals, and mindsets, and learned to walk alone without fear.

And now, at the end of this journey, you arrive at a truth that is both terrifying and exhilarating:

No one saves you. And that is good news.

It is good news because it means your life is yours, fully, completely, without reservation. No one else can dictate your victories, your failures, or your path forward. No one else holds the keys to your survival. You hold them. Every choice, every action, every moment of courage is yours alone.

It is good news because it means you are free to become who you truly are, unbound by expectation, unanchored by dependency, unafraid of abandonment. You are the architect, the warrior, the author, and the hero of your story.

It is good news because the world cannot break you unless you allow it. No one else has power over the core of your being, your will, your resolve, your capacity to act. Every external failure, every betrayal, every setback is merely a reflection of reality, not a verdict on your potential.

But good news also carries responsibility. It asks you to live deliberately, to act boldly, to carry yourself with integrity. Freedom without action is hollow. Strength without discipline is brittle. Awareness without effort is wasted.

So take this truth and carry it with courage. Let it guide you when the nights are long and the storms are fierce. Let it remind you that every time you rise, every time you act, every time you refuse to be rescued because you know you can save yourself, you are claiming a life that no one else can take from you.

No one saves you. And in that knowledge lies liberation, empowerment, and the raw, unshakable joy of standing fully in your own power.

Because when you realize that the only person who can save you is yourself, you also realize something extraordinary: you are enough. You have always been enough. And from this place, you can walk forward unafraid, knowing that you hold the greatest power in existence, the power to save your own life.

The End

About the Author

Dr. W. Koros writes with a gentle yet powerful voice, guiding readers toward inner strength, humility, and self-discovery. His books inspire people to pause, reflect, and uncover the quiet wisdom already within them.